Usborne Beginners
Caterpillars and butterflies

Stephanie Turnbull
Designed by Nelupa Hussain

Illustrated by Rosanne Guille and Uwe Mayer

Caterpillar and butterfly consultant: Michael Crosse,
The London Butterfly House

Reading consultant: Alison Kelly,
University of Surrey Roehampton

KU-092-256

Contents

L   4663 2

641960   SCH

J595.78

Amazing insects

Butterflies are flying insects with beautiful wings. They begin life as caterpillars.

This is a peacock butterfly. The spots on its wings look like the marks on a peacock's tail.

Tiny eggs

Butterflies lay eggs on leaves and twigs.

The eggs are sticky, so they don't fall off.

Some butterflies lay more than a thousand eggs in just a few weeks.

Many eggs have
a thick, rough covering.

A caterpillar is growing inside each egg.
They will be ready to hatch in a few days.

Butterfly eggs come in different shapes.

Some eggs
look like
round pearls.

Other eggs
are long
and thin.

A few hang
like beads
on a string.

Hatching out

A caterpillar bites a hole in its egg and wriggles out.

This cabbage white caterpillar is hatching. You can see other tiny caterpillars, still inside their eggs.

First a caterpillar eats its egg. This gives it energy.

It is still hungry, so it eats the leaf the egg was on.

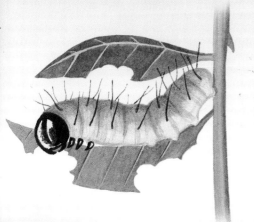

Then it moves on to eat more leaves from the same plant.

Caterpillars have strong jaws. They can munch through a leaf in seconds.

Lots of legs

All caterpillars have sixteen legs.

This is an emperor
gum moth caterpillar.

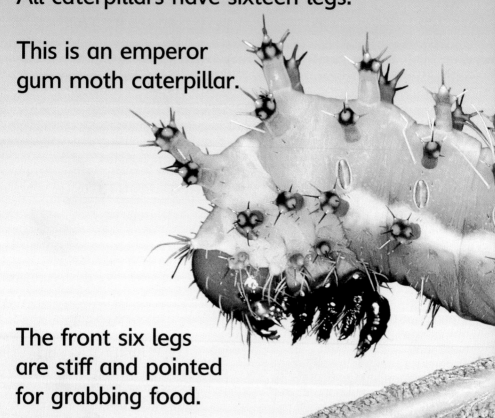

The front six legs
are stiff and pointed
for grabbing food.

The other legs are fatter.
They have suckers for
clinging onto stalks and twigs.

Some caterpillars move
along in big loops.

The front part
of the body
stretches out.

Then the
back part
lifts up...

and moves
up to meet
the front.

Stay away!

Birds and insects like to eat caterpillars. Many caterpillars have patterns on their body to help them hide.

This geometrid moth caterpillar looks just like a twig.

Some caterpillars make a horrible smell that keeps other animals away.

Many caterpillars try to look scary to frighten enemies.

Puss moth caterpillars rear up to look big and fierce.

Sweet oil caterpillars eat poisonous plants.

This makes them taste bad to birds.

11

Big eaters

Caterpillars eat all the time. They find a plant they like, and eat until it is all gone.

These caterpillars are called large whites. They only like to eat cabbage leaves.

Caterpillars soon grow so fat that their skin is too tight and starts to split.

They wriggle out of the old skin. Underneath is a new, stretchy skin.

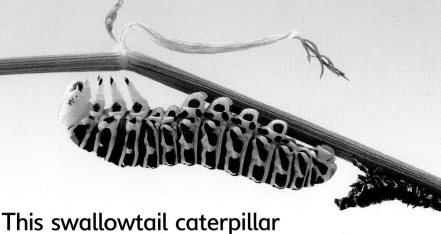

This swallowtail caterpillar has a brand new skin. It leaves the old skin behind.

Most caterpillars change their skin four times. Each time, the patterns are more interesting.

Time to change

Soon, caterpillars are ready to turn into butterflies.

1. First a caterpillar finds a safe, sheltered place.

2. It hangs upside down using hooks on its body.

3. Its skin splits and falls off. Underneath is a new skin.

4. The skin gets harder and harder until it is like a case.

The hard case is called a pupa.

A pupa hangs without moving for weeks. Inside, a butterfly is growing.

Some caterpillars hide inside a rolled-up leaf before they turn into a pupa.

A new body

When butterflies are fully grown, they are ready to break out of their pupa.

You can see this butterfly's wings inside its pupa.

A butterfly slowly pushes itself out of its pupa.

16

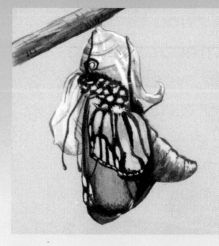

Then it stops to rest. Its wings are pale, damp and crumpled.

Butterflies have to let their wings dry out before they can fly.

This monarch butterfly must wait a few hours for its wings to spread out and get stiffer.

Butterflies don't grow after they have hatched. They stay the same size all their lives.

Up and away

Butterflies are always moving around. They never stay still for long.

All butterflies have four big, wide wings.

They flap all four wings together.

The wings are covered in tiny scales. You can see them under a microscope.

Scale———

Some butterflies flap their wings 70 times every second.

What is a moth?

A moth looks a lot like a butterfly, but it is not quite the same.

This emperor moth has smaller, narrower wings than a butterfly.

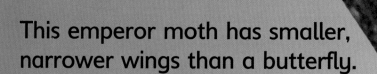

Hawk moths can fly much faster than you can run!

Most moths fly at night, when there are not so many enemies around.

This is a Madagascan moon moth.

Moths have fat, furry bodies to keep them warm on cold nights.

They have feathery feelers that sense objects in the dark.

Feeding

Butterflies and moths feed on juices from flowers or fruit. Instead of a mouth, they have a long, thin tube called a proboscis.

They drink through it like a straw.

Asian vampire moths can prick an animal's skin and drink its blood.

The proboscis is usually curled up.

It uncurls when the butterfly drinks.

When butterflies are thirsty, they often suck up drops of water from damp ground.

Vanishing act

Lots of animals like to eat butterflies. Some butterflies have patterns that help them hide.

If this leaf butterfly keeps still, enemies think it is just a leaf.

Glasswing butterflies have see-through wings, which makes them hard to spot.

This hairstreak butterfly is easy to see as it flies.

Its wings are green underneath, so it can hide when it lands.

This orange tip butterfly looks like the flowers it feeds on.

Showing off

Some butterflies are poisonous, so they don't need to hide from enemies.

Bright markings on this swallowtail butterfly warn animals that it tastes bad.

Some butterflies have big spots like eyes on their wings to make them look scary.

These butterflies both look poisonous to animals, but the one on the left is harmless. It copies the poisonous butterfly's patterns.

This moth has a fat body and small wings. Enemies think it is a bee and leave it alone.

Big and small

Butterflies and moths come in all shapes and sizes.

Atlas moths are the biggest moths in the world. Each of their wings is wider than a page of this book.

 The smallest butterfly is called a pygmy blue. This is its real size.

This is
a zebra
swallowtail
butterfly.

Many swallowtails
have long wings
that make them
look bigger.

This helps to protect them from enemies.

Birds often snap
at the butterfly's
dangling tails
instead of its body.

The butterfly has
a chance to escape.
Losing a bit of its
wing doesn't hurt.

Glossary of butterfly words

Here are some of the words in this book you might not know. This page tells you what they mean.

 sucker - a sticky pad on a caterpillar's leg. Suckers help caterpillars grip stalks.

 pupa - a hard case that forms around a caterpillar as it changes into a butterfly.

 scales - the tiny, flat flakes that cover a butterfly's wings.

 moth - an insect with wings that looks a lot like a butterfly.

 feelers - stalks on a butterfly's head that sense smells and sounds.

 proboscis - a butterfly's long tongue, used for drinking liquids.

 poisonous - something that is dangerous to eat. Some butterflies are poisonous.

Web sites to visit

If you have a computer, you can find out more about caterpillars and butterflies on the Internet. On the Usborne Quicklinks Web site there are links to four Web sites.

Web site 1 - Print out caterpillar and butterfly pictures to crayon.

Web site 2 - Match the butterfly pairs in a memory game.

Web site 3 - See speeded-up film showing the stages in the life of a monarch butterfly.

Web site 4 - Solve a butterfly puzzle.

To visit these Web sites, go to **www.usborne-quicklinks.com** and type the keywords "beginners caterpillars". Then click on the link for the Web site you want to visit. Before you use the Internet, look at the safety guidelines inside the back cover of this book and ask an adult to read them with you.

Index

Acknowledgements

Managing editor: Fiona Watt, Managing designer: Mary Cartwright

Photographic manipulation by John Russell and Emma Julings

With thanks to Michelle Lawrence

Photo credits

The publishers are grateful to the following for permission to reproduce material:
© **Alamy:** 18-19 & 31 (Gay Bumgarner); © **Ardea:** 2-3 (Jack M. Bailey), 15 & 20 (John Mason), 27 (Alan Weaving), 29 (Elizabeth S. Burgess); © **Corbis:** Cover (Gary W. Carter), 4 (Michael & Patricia Fogden), 25 (Laura Sivell; Papilio), 26 (George D. Lepp); © **FLPA/Minden Pictures:** 12 (Ray Bird), 16 (S & D & K Maslowski), 21 (Frans Lanting), 28m (C. Mullen); © **Getty Images:** 1 (Gail Shumway), 8-9 (David Maitland); © **Oxford Scientific Films:** 5 (David M. Dennis), 6, 10 (David M. Dennis); © **Science Photo Library:** 11 & 19 (Claude Nuridsany & Marie Perennou); © **James F. Snyder:** 28b; © **Still Pictures:** 24 (Luiz C. Marigo); © **Warren Photographic:** 13, 17, 22, 23 (all Kim Taylor)

Every effort has been made to trace and acknowledge ownership of copyright. If any rights have been omitted, the publishers offer to rectify this in any subsequent editions following notification.

First published in 2003 by Usborne Publishing Ltd., Usborne House, 83-85 Saffron Hill, London EC1N 8RT, England. www.usborne.com Copyright © 2003 Usborne Publishing Ltd. The name Usborne and the devices ♀ ⊕ are Trade Marks of Usborne Publishing Ltd. All rights reserved. No part of this publication may be reproduced, stored in a retrieval system, or transmitted in any form or by any means, electronic, mechanical, photocopying, recording or otherwise without the prior permission of the publisher. First published in America 2003. U.E. Printed in Belgium.

Internet safety rules

- Ask your parent's or guardian's permission before you connect to the Internet.

- When you are on the Internet, never tell anyone your full name, address or telephone number, and ask an adult before you give your e-mail address.

- If a Web site asks you to log in or register by typing your name or e-mail address, ask an adult's permission first.

- If you do receive an e-mail from someone you don't know, tell an adult and do not reply to the e-mail.

Notes for parents or guardians

The Web sites described in this book are regularly reviewed and the links in Usborne Quicklinks are updated. However, the content of a Web site may change at any time and Usborne Publishing is not responsible, and does not accept liability, for the content or availability of any Web site other than its own, or for any exposure to harmful, offensive or inaccurate material which may appear on the Web. We recommend that children are supervised while on the Internet, that they do not use Internet Chat Rooms and that you use Internet filtering software to block unsuitable material. Please ensure that your children follow the safety guidelines printed above. For more information, see the "Net Help" area on the Usborne Quicklinks Web site at **www.usborne-quicklinks.com**